Empanada Cookbook

A Delicious Journey into the World of Savory Stuffed Pastries

While every precaution has been taken in the preparation of this book, the publisher assumes no responsibility for errors or omissions, or for damages resulting from the use of the information contained herein.

EMPANADA COOKBOOK

First edition. January 18, 2024.

Copyright © 2024 Sammy Andrews.

ISBN: 979-8224019427

Written by Sammy Andrews.

Table of Contents

Sammy Andrews

Chapter 1: Introduction to Empanadas

History and Origins

Empanadas, those delectable savory pastries filled with a variety of fillings, have a rich and diverse history that spans across continents and cultures. The term "empanada" itself comes from the Spanish verb "empanar," which means "to coat or wrap in bread." While the origins of empanadas can be traced back to Spain, they have evolved into unique and beloved creations in countries all over the world.

Spain: The Birthplace of Empanadas

The story of empanadas begins in Spain, where they are believed to have been created during the Moorish rule of the Iberian Peninsula. In the Spanish region of Galicia, you'll find the "empanada gallega," a large, round pastry often filled with seafood, meats, or vegetables. These empanadas were initially made as a way to preserve and transport food during long journeys or as a convenient snack for farmers working in the fields.

Latin America: Empanadas with a Twist

Empanadas made their way to Latin America through Spanish colonization. Each Latin American country has put its own unique spin on these delightful pastries, resulting in a wide array of flavors and ingredients. In Argentina, for example, empanadas are a national treasure, with distinct regional variations. Chileans love their "empanadas de pino," filled with ground beef, onions, olives, and hard-boiled eggs, while Venezuelans savor "empanadas de carne mechada" filled with slow-cooked, shredded beef.

Other Global Variations

Beyond Spain and Latin America, empanadas have found their way into the culinary traditions of countries such as the Philippines, India, and Jamaica. Filipino empanadas are often stuffed with a mixture of ground meat, vegetables, and sometimes even sweet ingredients like banana or jackfruit. In India, the influence of empanadas can be seen in the popular street food "samosa," a deep-fried pastry filled with spiced potatoes and peas.

Variations Around the World

Empanadas come in all shapes, sizes, and flavors, and exploring the diverse world of empanadas is a delightful culinary adventure. Here are a few examples of empanada variations from different parts of the globe:

Cornish Pasty (England)

The Cornish pasty bears a striking resemblance to the empanada. It's a pastry filled with meat, potatoes, and vegetables, traditionally associated with Cornwall, England. The idea of a portable, pastry-encased meal is a common thread in many cultures.

Sambusak (Middle East)

In Middle Eastern cuisine, you'll find the sambusak, a savory pastry often filled with spiced meats, vegetables, or cheese. These delicious hand pies have been enjoyed for centuries across the region.

Samosa (India)

The Indian samosa is a close cousin to the empanada, featuring a crispy pastry shell filled with various fillings, such as spiced potatoes, peas, and sometimes minced meat. Samosas are a beloved street food and snack in India and beyond.

Tools and Ingredients

Before you embark on your empanada-making journey, it's important to have the right tools and ingredients on hand. Here's a basic list to get you started:

Tools:

- Rolling pin
- Pastry brush
- Baking sheets
- Mixing bowls
- Fork or pastry crimper (for sealing the edges)

Ingredients:

- Empanada dough (homemade or store-bought)
- Filling ingredients (varies depending on the recipe)
- Olive oil or cooking spray (for brushing the empanadas)
- Optional: egg wash (for a shiny, golden crust)

Empanada-Making Tips

As you dive into making empanadas, keep these tips in mind:

Choose the Right Dough: Select the type of empanada dough that suits your preference and recipe. Whether it's a flaky pastry or a dough with a more bread-like texture, the choice of dough can significantly impact the final product.

Filling Balance: Ensure a good balance of flavors and textures in your filling. Consider the interplay of savory and sweet, crunchy and tender, and experiment with seasonings to create the perfect combination.

Sealing Techniques: Learn the art of sealing your empanadas properly to prevent fillings from leaking during baking. You can use a fork to crimp the edges or try decorative techniques for a professional touch.

Don't Overfill: Avoid overstuffing your empanadas, as this can lead to difficulty sealing them and a messy outcome. Follow the recipe guidelines for filling quantity.

Even Cooking: Arrange your empanadas evenly on the baking sheet, ensuring they have enough space between them for even cooking. Rotate the tray if necessary to achieve consistent browning.

Now that you have a glimpse into the world of empanadas, you're ready to embark on your culinary journey. In the following chapters, we'll explore a wide range of empanada recipes, from classic favorites to international delights. Get ready to roll out the dough, fill the pastries, and savor the delicious results.

Chapter 2: Empanada Dough Basics

In the world of empanadas, the dough is the canvas upon which you create your culinary masterpieces. Understanding the different types of empanada dough and mastering the techniques of making and handling it are essential for crafting perfect empanadas. In this chapter, we'll delve into the fundamentals of empanada dough.

Types of Empanada Dough

Empanada dough can vary in texture, flavor, and ingredients, and each type of dough lends a unique character to your creations. Here are some common types of empanada dough:

1. Traditional Shortcrust Dough

Shortcrust dough, also known as pie dough, is a classic choice for empanadas. It's flaky, buttery, and wonderfully tender. This dough type is made with flour, butter, water, and a pinch of salt. It's versatile and can be used for both savory and sweet empanadas.

2. Yeast-Risen Dough

Yeast-risen empanada dough is slightly more bread-like in texture. It's made with yeast, flour, water, salt, and sometimes a touch of sugar. This dough requires rising time, but it yields empanadas with a soft, airy interior.

3. Cornmeal Dough

Cornmeal dough, often called "masa harina," is a popular choice for South American empanadas. It's made from cornmeal, water, and a little fat (such as oil or lard). This dough has a distinct flavor and is commonly used for savory empanadas.

4. Phyllo Dough

Phyllo dough is paper-thin and results in exceptionally crispy empanadas. While it's not a traditional choice, it can be used for a unique twist on these pastries. Brush each layer of phyllo with melted butter or oil before folding.

5. Puff Pastry

Puff pastry creates empanadas with a flaky, layered texture. It's a convenient option when you're short on time, as it's readily available in stores. Be sure to thaw it properly before using, and handle it gently to maintain its flakiness.

Making Homemade Dough

If you're up for the challenge, making your own empanada dough from scratch can be a rewarding experience. Here's a basic recipe for homemade shortcrust dough, which can be used for a wide range of empanadas:

Ingredients:

- 2 1/2 cups all-purpose flour
- 1 cup (2 sticks) unsalted butter, cold and cubed
- 1/2 teaspoon salt
- 1/2 cup ice water

Instructions:

In a large mixing bowl, combine the flour and salt.

Add the cold, cubed butter to the flour mixture. Use a pastry cutter or your fingertips to work the butter into the flour until the mixture resembles coarse crumbs.

Gradually add the ice water, a few tablespoons at a time, and mix until the dough just comes together. Be careful not to overwork the dough.

Divide the dough into two equal portions, shape them into discs, and wrap them in plastic wrap. Refrigerate for at least 30 minutes before rolling out.

Working with Store-Bought Dough

Using store-bought empanada dough is a convenient option when you're short on time or want a hassle-free experience. Follow these steps when working with store-bought dough:

Thaw Properly: If you're using frozen dough, follow the instructions on the packaging for thawing. Usually, it involves letting the dough sit in the refrigerator for several hours or overnight.

Handle Gently: Store-bought dough can be delicate, so handle it with care. Roll it out on a lightly floured surface, and use a rolling pin to achieve the desired thickness.

Cutting and Shaping: Cut the dough into circles or squares, depending on your empanada shape preference. Place the filling in the center and fold the dough over, sealing the edges.

Sealing: Press the edges of the dough together firmly to seal the empanada. You can use a fork to create a decorative pattern or simply crimp the edges with your fingers.

Rolling and Shaping Techniques

The way you roll and shape your empanada dough can influence the final appearance and texture of your empanadas. Here are a few techniques to consider:

1. Circular Empanadas

- Roll out the dough into a large circle.
- Use a round cutter or a small plate as a guide to cut out circles.
- Place the filling in the center of each circle, then fold it in half, creating a half-moon shape.
- Seal the edges by crimping with a fork or by folding and twisting the edges to create a rope-like pattern.

2. Square Empanadas

- Roll out the dough into a rectangle.
- Cut the dough into equal-sized squares.

- Place the filling in the center of each square, then fold it diagonally, creating a triangle shape.
- Seal the edges by pressing with your fingers or a fork.

3. Decorative Edges

- To give your empanadas an artistic touch, experiment with decorative edge patterns. You can fold, twist, or braid the edges for a visually appealing finish.

With these dough basics under your belt, you're well-prepared to move on to creating a wide variety of empanada recipes. Whether you choose to make your own dough or use store-bought options, the possibilities are endless. In the following chapters, we'll explore different empanada recipes that showcase various dough types and filling combinations.

Chapter 3: Classic Beef Empanadas

Ingredients

For the Filling:

- 1 pound ground beef
- 1 medium onion, finely chopped
- 2 cloves garlic, minced
- 1/2 red bell pepper, finely chopped
- 1/2 green bell pepper, finely chopped
- 1/2 teaspoon cumin
- 1/2 teaspoon paprika
- 1/4 teaspoon chili powder (adjust to taste)
- Salt and black pepper to taste
- 1/4 cup green olives, pitted and chopped
- 2 hard-boiled eggs, chopped
- 2 tablespoons raisins (optional)
- 2 tablespoons olive oil

For the Dough (Short crust):

- 2 1/2 cups all-purpose flour
- 1 cup (2 sticks) unsalted butter, cold and cubed
- 1/2 teaspoon salt
- 1/2 cup ice water

Filling Preparation

Heat the olive oil in a large skillet over medium heat. Add the chopped onions and garlic and sauté until they become translucent and fragrant.

Add the ground beef to the skillet and cook, breaking it apart with a spatula, until it's browned and fully cooked.

Stir in the red and green bell peppers and continue to cook for another 2-3 minutes until they soften.

Season the mixture with cumin, paprika, chili powder, salt, and black pepper. Adjust the spices to your taste preferences.

Remove the skillet from heat and stir in the chopped green olives, hard-boiled eggs, and raisins (if using). This filling should have a balance of savory, salty, and slightly sweet flavors.

Allow the filling to cool to room temperature before using it in your empanadas.

Dough Handling

If you're making your own dough, follow the instructions in Chapter 2 for making shortcrust dough. Divide the dough into equal portions and roll them into small balls.

Roll out each dough ball into a thin circle, about 6-8 inches in diameter. You can use a rolling pin and a lightly floured surface for this step.

Place a spoonful of the beef filling in the center of each dough circle.

Fold the dough over the filling, creating a half-moon shape. Press the edges firmly to seal the empanada. You can use a fork to crimp the edges for a decorative touch.

Repeat this process for the remaining dough and filling.

Baking and Serving

Preheat your oven to 375°F (190°C).

Place the empanadas on a baking sheet lined with parchment paper, leaving some space between them to allow for even baking.

If desired, you can brush the tops of the empanadas with an egg wash (a beaten egg with a tablespoon of water) for a shiny, golden crust.

Bake the empanadas in the preheated oven for 20-25 minutes or until they are golden brown and crisp.

Allow the empanadas to cool slightly before serving. They can be served warm as an appetizer, snack, or main course.

Empanadas are often enjoyed with dipping sauces such as chimichurri or a simple tomato salsa.

These classic beef empanadas are a crowd-pleaser and make for a satisfying and flavorful meal. Whether you're serving them at a family gathering or as a quick weeknight dinner, the combination of savory beef filling and flaky pastry is sure to be a hit.

Chapter 4: Chicken and Cheese Empanadas

Ingredients

For the Filling:

- 1 pound boneless, skinless chicken breasts, cooked and shredded
- 1 cup shredded mozzarella cheese
- 1/2 cup cream cheese
- 1/2 cup corn kernels (fresh or frozen)
- 1/4 cup chopped fresh cilantro
- 1/4 cup red onion, finely chopped
- 2 cloves garlic, minced
- 1 teaspoon ground cumin
- 1/2 teaspoon chili powder
- Salt and black pepper to taste
- 2 tablespoons olive oil

For the Dough (Short crust):

- 2 1/2 cups all-purpose flour
- 1 cup (2 sticks) unsalted butter, cold and cubed
- 1/2 teaspoon salt
- 1/2 cup ice water

Filling Preparation

In a large skillet, heat the olive oil over medium heat. Add the chopped red onion and garlic, and sauté until they become translucent and aromatic.

Add the shredded chicken to the skillet and cook for a few minutes until it's heated through.

Stir in the cream cheese, mozzarella cheese, corn kernels, chopped cilantro, ground cumin, chili powder, salt, and black pepper. Mix everything together until the cheeses melt and the filling is well combined. Remove it from the heat and let it cool slightly.

Taste the filling and adjust the seasonings to your liking. You can add more salt, pepper, or spices as needed.

Dough Handling

If you're making your own dough, follow the instructions in Chapter 2 for making short crust dough. Divide the dough into equal portions and roll them into small balls.

Roll out each dough ball into a thin circle, approximately 6-8 inches in diameter, using a rolling pin and a lightly floured surface.

Place a spoonful of the chicken and cheese filling in the center of each dough circle.

Fold the dough over the filling, creating a half-moon shape. Press the edges firmly to seal the empanada. You can use a fork to crimp the edges for a decorative touch.

Repeat this process for the remaining dough and filling.

Baking and Serving

Preheat your oven to 375°F (190°C).

Place the chicken and cheese empanadas on a baking sheet lined with parchment paper, ensuring there is some space between them for even baking.

If desired, you can brush the tops of the empanadas with an egg wash (a beaten egg with a tablespoon of water) for a shiny, golden crust.

Bake the empanadas in the preheated oven for 20-25 minutes or until they are golden brown and the filling is hot and bubbly.

Allow the empanadas to cool for a few minutes before serving. They are best enjoyed warm.

Consider serving these empanadas with a side of salsa, sour cream, or guacamole for dipping.

Chicken and cheese empanadas are a delightful combination of tender, seasoned chicken and creamy, melted cheese, all enclosed in a flaky pastry shell. They make for a fantastic appetizer, party snack, or even a satisfying meal when paired with a fresh salad.

Chapter 5: Vegetarian Delights: Spinach and Feta Empanadas

Ingredients

For the Filling:

- 2 cups fresh spinach leaves, chopped
- 1 cup crumbled feta cheese
- 1/2 cup ricotta cheese
- 1/4 cup finely chopped red onion
- 2 cloves garlic, minced
- 1/4 cup grated Parmesan cheese
- 1/4 teaspoon ground nutmeg
- Salt and black pepper to taste
- 2 tablespoons olive oil

For the Dough (Short crust):

- 2 1/2 cups all-purpose flour
- 1 cup (2 sticks) unsalted butter, cold and cubed
- 1/2 teaspoon salt
- 1/2 cup ice water

Filling Preparation

In a large skillet, heat the olive oil over medium heat. Add the minced garlic and chopped red onion, and sauté until they become fragrant and the onion turns translucent.

Add the chopped spinach to the skillet and cook for a few minutes until it wilts and becomes tender. Remove the skillet from the heat.

In a mixing bowl, combine the crumbled feta cheese, ricotta cheese, grated Parmesan cheese, ground nutmeg, and the sautéed spinach mixture. Mix everything together until well combined. Season with salt and black pepper to taste.

Taste the filling and adjust the seasonings if needed. Keep in mind that feta cheese can be salty, so you may not need much additional salt.

Dough Handling

If you're making your own dough, follow the instructions in Chapter 2 for making short crust dough. Divide the dough into equal portions and roll them into small balls.

Roll out each dough ball into a thin circle, approximately 6-8 inches in diameter, using a rolling pin and a lightly floured surface.

Place a spoonful of the spinach and feta filling in the center of each dough circle.

Fold the dough over the filling, creating a half-moon shape. Press the edges firmly to seal the empanada. You can use a fork to crimp the edges for a decorative touch.

Repeat this process for the remaining dough and filling.

Baking and Serving

Preheat your oven to 375°F (190°C).

Place the spinach and feta empanadas on a baking sheet lined with parchment paper, ensuring there is some space between them for even baking.

If desired, you can brush the tops of the empanadas with an egg wash (a beaten egg with a tablespoon of water) for a shiny, golden crust.

Bake the empanadas in the preheated oven for 20-25 minutes or until they are golden brown and the filling is hot and creamy.

Allow the empanadas to cool for a few minutes before serving. They are best enjoyed warm.

Consider serving these vegetarian delights with a side of tzatziki sauce or a fresh Greek salad for a Mediterranean-inspired meal.

Spinach and feta empanadas are a wonderful vegetarian option filled with the savory goodness of wilted spinach and the creamy tang of feta and ricotta cheeses. These empanadas are perfect for those looking for a meatless alternative that's still packed with flavor.

Chapter 6: Seafood Sensations: Shrimp and Scallop Empanadas

Ingredients

For the Filling:

- 1/2 pound large shrimp, peeled, deveined, and chopped
- 1/2 pound sea scallops, chopped
- 1/2 cup diced red bell pepper
- 1/2 cup diced green bell pepper
- 1/2 cup diced onion
- 2 cloves garlic, minced
- 1/4 cup fresh cilantro, chopped
- 1/4 cup fresh parsley, chopped
- Juice of 1 lime
- 1/2 teaspoon paprika
- 1/4 teaspoon cayenne pepper (adjust to taste)
- Salt and black pepper to taste
- 2 tablespoons olive oil

For the Dough (Short crust):

- 2 1/2 cups all-purpose flour
- 1 cup (2 sticks) unsalted butter, cold and cubed
- 1/2 teaspoon salt
- 1/2 cup ice water

Filling Preparation

In a large skillet, heat the olive oil over medium-high heat. Add the minced garlic and diced onion, and sauté until they become translucent and aromatic.

Add the chopped red and green bell peppers to the skillet and sauté for a few minutes until they begin to soften.

Stir in the chopped shrimp and scallops, and cook for 2-3 minutes until they start to turn opaque.

Add the paprika, cayenne pepper, salt, and black pepper to the skillet. Mix well to coat the seafood and vegetables with the spices.

Continue cooking for another 2-3 minutes until the shrimp and scallops are fully cooked and have a light pink color.

Remove the skillet from the heat and stir in the chopped cilantro, chopped parsley, and lime juice. Adjust the seasoning to your taste.

Allow the seafood filling to cool to room temperature before using it in your empanadas.

Dough Handling

If you're making your own dough, follow the instructions in Chapter 2 for making shortcrust dough. Divide the dough into equal portions and roll them into small balls.

Roll out each dough ball into a thin circle, approximately 6-8 inches in diameter, using a rolling pin and a lightly floured surface.

Place a spoonful of the seafood filling in the center of each dough circle.

Fold the dough over the filling, creating a half-moon shape. Press the edges firmly to seal the empanada. You can use a fork to crimp the edges for a decorative touch.

Repeat this process for the remaining dough and filling.

Baking and Serving

Preheat your oven to 375°F (190°C).

Place the shrimp and scallop empanadas on a baking sheet lined with parchment paper, ensuring there is some space between them for even baking.

If desired, you can brush the tops of the empanadas with an egg wash (a beaten egg with a tablespoon of water) for a shiny, golden crust.

Bake the empanadas in the preheated oven for 20-25 minutes or until they are golden brown and the seafood filling is hot and flavorful.

Allow the empanadas to cool for a few minutes before serving. They are best enjoyed warm.

Consider serving these seafood sensations with a side of citrus aioli or a simple mixed greens salad for a refreshing complement.

Shrimp and scallop empanadas offer a taste of the ocean with succulent seafood and a medley of fresh herbs and spices.

Chapter 7: Breakfast Empanadas: Sausage and Egg

Ingredients

For the Filling:

- 1/2 pound breakfast sausage, cooked and crumbled
- 4 large eggs, scrambled
- 1/2 cup shredded cheddar cheese
- 1/4 cup chopped green onions
- Salt and black pepper to taste
- 2 tablespoons olive oil

For the Dough (Short crust):

- 2 1/2 cups all-purpose flour
- 1 cup (2 sticks) unsalted butter, cold and cubed
- 1/2 teaspoon salt
- 1/2 cup ice water

Filling Preparation

In a large skillet, heat the olive oil over medium heat. Add the cooked breakfast sausage and sauté for a few minutes to warm it through.

In a separate pan, scramble the eggs until they are just set but still slightly moist. Season them with salt and black pepper to taste.

Combine the scrambled eggs, crumbled sausage, shredded cheddar cheese, and chopped green onions in a mixing bowl. Mix everything together until the filling is well combined.

Taste the filling and adjust the seasoning if necessary.

Dough Handling

If you're making your own dough, follow the instructions in Chapter 2 for making short crust dough. Divide the dough into equal portions and roll them into small balls.

Roll out each dough ball into a thin circle, approximately 6-8 inches in diameter, using a rolling pin and a lightly floured surface.

Place a spoonful of the sausage and egg filling in the center of each dough circle.

Fold the dough over the filling, creating a half-moon shape. Press the edges firmly to seal the empanada. You can use a fork to crimp the edges for a decorative touch.

Repeat this process for the remaining dough and filling.

Baking and Serving

Preheat your oven to 375°F (190°C).

Place the breakfast empanadas on a baking sheet lined with parchment paper, making sure there is some space between them for even baking.

If desired, you can brush the tops of the empanadas with an egg wash (a beaten egg with a tablespoon of water) for a shiny, golden crust.

Bake the empanadas in the preheated oven for 20-25 minutes or until they are golden brown and the filling is hot and cheesy.

Allow the empanadas to cool for a few minutes before serving. They are best enjoyed warm.

Consider serving these breakfast empanadas with a side of salsa or ketchup for dipping, and perhaps a cup of hot coffee or tea for a complete morning meal.

Breakfast empanadas filled with savory sausage, scrambled eggs, and melted cheddar cheese are a delightful way to start your day. These portable breakfast treats are perfect for busy mornings, brunch gatherings, or as a grab-and-go option when you're on the move.

Chapter 8: Sweet Potato and Black Bean Empanadas

Ingredients

For the Filling:

- 2 medium sweet potatoes, peeled and diced into small cubes
- 1 can (15 ounces) black beans, drained and rinsed
- 1 cup diced red bell pepper
- 1 cup diced red onion
- 2 cloves garlic, minced
- 1 teaspoon ground cumin
- 1/2 teaspoon smoked paprika
- Salt and black pepper to taste
- 2 tablespoons olive oil

For the Dough (Short crust):

- 2 1/2 cups all-purpose flour
- 1 cup (2 sticks) unsalted butter, cold and cubed
- 1/2 teaspoon salt
- 1/2 cup ice water

Filling Preparation

Preheat your oven to 375°F (190°C).

Place the diced sweet potatoes on a baking sheet lined with parchment paper. Drizzle them with olive oil, and sprinkle with salt and black pepper to taste. Toss to coat evenly.

Roast the sweet potatoes in the preheated oven for about 20-25 minutes, or until they are tender and slightly caramelized. Remove them from the oven and set aside.

In a large skillet, heat a bit of olive oil over medium heat. Add the minced garlic, diced red onion, and diced red bell pepper. Sauté until they become softened and aromatic.

Add the drained black beans to the skillet, along with the roasted sweet potatoes. Season with ground cumin, smoked paprika, salt, and black pepper. Stir well to combine all the ingredients.

Cook the filling for a few more minutes, allowing the flavors to meld. Taste and adjust the seasonings as needed.

Remove the filling from the heat and let it cool to room temperature before using it for your empanadas.

Dough Handling

If you're making your own dough, follow the instructions in Chapter 2 for making short crust dough. Divide the dough into equal portions and roll them into small balls.

Roll out each dough ball into a thin circle, approximately 6-8 inches in diameter, using a rolling pin and a lightly floured surface.

Place a spoonful of the sweet potato and black bean filling in the center of each dough circle.

Fold the dough over the filling, creating a half-moon shape. Press the edges firmly to seal the empanada. You can use a fork to crimp the edges for a decorative touch.

Repeat this process for the remaining dough and filling.

Baking and Serving

Preheat your oven to 375°F (190°C).

Place the sweet potato and black bean empanadas on a baking sheet lined with parchment paper, ensuring there is some space between them for even baking.

If desired, you can brush the tops of the empanadas with an egg wash (a beaten egg with a tablespoon of water) for a shiny, golden crust.

Bake the empanadas in the preheated oven for 20-25 minutes or until they are golden brown and the filling is hot and flavorful.

Allow the empanadas to cool for a few minutes before serving. They are best enjoyed warm.

Consider serving these empanadas with a dollop of sour cream or a drizzle of your favorite hot sauce for a burst of flavor.

Sweet potato and black bean empanadas offer a delightful combination of earthy sweetness from roasted sweet potatoes and the heartiness of black beans. These empanadas are not only delicious but also a great option for vegetarians and vegans looking for a flavorful meal.

Chapter 9: Cheese Lover's Paradise: Queso Blanco Empanadas

Ingredients

For the Filling:

- 2 cups queso blanco cheese, diced into small cubes
- 1/2 cup queso fresco cheese, crumbled
- 1/4 cup cream cheese
- 1/4 cup diced green chilies (mild or hot, depending on your preference)
- 1/4 cup finely chopped fresh cilantro
- 2 cloves garlic, minced
- Salt and black pepper to taste
- 2 tablespoons olive oil

For the Dough (Short crust):

- 2 1/2 cups all-purpose flour
- 1 cup (2 sticks) unsalted butter, cold and cubed
- 1/2 teaspoon salt
- 1/2 cup ice water

Filling Preparation

In a mixing bowl, combine the diced queso blanco cheese, crumbled queso fresco cheese, and cream cheese. Mix until the cheeses are well incorporated.

In a skillet, heat the olive oil over medium heat. Add the minced garlic and diced green chilies. Sauté for a couple of minutes until they become fragrant.

Remove the skillet from heat and let the garlic and chilies cool slightly.

Add the sautéed garlic and chilies to the cheese mixture. Stir in the finely chopped cilantro. Season with salt and black pepper to taste.

Taste the filling and adjust the seasonings if needed. Keep in mind that the cheese can vary in saltiness, so adjust accordingly.

Dough Handling

If you're making your own dough, follow the instructions in Chapter 2 for making short crust dough. Divide the dough into equal portions and roll them into small balls.

Roll out each dough ball into a thin circle, approximately 6-8 inches in diameter, using a rolling pin and a lightly floured surface.

Place a generous spoonful of the queso blanco cheese filling in the center of each dough circle.

Fold the dough over the filling, creating a half-moon shape. Press the edges firmly to seal the empanada. You can use a fork to crimp the edges for a decorative touch.

Repeat this process for the remaining dough and filling.

Baking and Serving

Preheat your oven to 375°F (190°C).

Place the queso Blanco empanadas on a baking sheet lined with parchment paper, ensuring there is some space between them for even baking.

If desired, you can brush the tops of the empanadas with an egg wash (a beaten egg with a tablespoon of water) for a shiny, golden crust.

Bake the empanadas in the preheated oven for 20-25 minutes or until they are golden brown and the cheese filling is hot and gooey.

Allow the empanadas to cool for a few minutes before serving. They are best enjoyed warm.

Consider serving these cheesy delights with a side of salsa Verde or a simple tomato salsa for dipping.

Queso Blanco empanadas are a cheese lover's dream, featuring a rich and creamy filling made with a blend of cheeses and a touch of heat from green chilies. These empanadas are perfect for parties, snacks, or whenever you're craving a cheesy indulgence.

Chapter 10: Spicy Jalapeño and Cheddar Empanadas

Ingredients

For the Filling:

- 2 cups shredded sharp cheddar cheese
- 1/2 cup diced pickled jalapeños (adjust to your spice preference)
- 1/4 cup diced red onion
- 1/4 cup diced red bell pepper
- 1/4 cup diced green bell pepper
- 2 cloves garlic, minced
- 1/4 cup chopped fresh cilantro
- 1 teaspoon ground cumin
- Salt and black pepper to taste
- 2 tablespoons olive oil

For the Dough (Short crust):

- 2 1/2 cups all-purpose flour
- 1 cup (2 sticks) unsalted butter, cold and cubed
- 1/2 teaspoon salt
- 1/2 cup ice water

Filling Preparation

In a mixing bowl, combine the shredded sharp cheddar cheese, diced pickled jalapeños, diced red onion, diced red bell pepper, and diced green bell pepper. Mix until the ingredients are evenly distributed.

In a skillet, heat the olive oil over medium heat. Add the minced garlic and sauté for about 30 seconds until it becomes fragrant.

Remove the skillet from heat and let the garlic cool slightly.

Add the sautéed garlic to the cheese and pepper mixture. Stir in the chopped fresh cilantro, ground cumin, salt, and black pepper. Mix well to combine.

Taste the filling and adjust the seasonings, especially the spiciness level, according to your preference.

Dough Handling

If you're making your own dough, follow the instructions in Chapter 2 for making short crust dough. Divide the dough into equal portions and roll them into small balls.

Roll out each dough ball into a thin circle, approximately 6-8 inches in diameter, using a rolling pin and a lightly floured surface.

Place a spoonful of the spicy jalapeño and cheddar filling in the center of each dough circle.

Fold the dough over the filling, creating a half-moon shape. Press the edges firmly to seal the empanada. You can use a fork to crimp the edges for a decorative touch.

Repeat this process for the remaining dough and filling.

Baking and Serving

Preheat your oven to 375°F (190°C).

Place the spicy jalapeño and cheddar empanadas on a baking sheet lined with parchment paper, ensuring there is some space between them for even baking.

If desired, you can brush the tops of the empanadas with an egg wash (a beaten egg with a tablespoon of water) for a shiny, golden crust.

Bake the empanadas in the preheated oven for 20-25 minutes or until they are golden brown and the cheese filling is hot and gooey.

Allow the empanadas to cool for a few minutes before serving. They are best enjoyed warm.

Consider serving these spicy delights with a side of sour cream or a cooling avocado dip to balance the heat.

Spicy jalapeño and cheddar empanadas offer a fiery kick from pickled jalapeños and the creamy goodness of sharp cheddar cheese. These empanadas are perfect for those who crave a bold and zesty flavor experience.

Chapter 11: Exotic Fillings: Lamb and Mint Empanadas

Ingredients

For the Filling:

- 1 pound ground lamb
- 1/2 cup diced red onion
- 1/4 cup finely chopped fresh mint leaves
- 2 cloves garlic, minced
- 1/4 cup diced tomatoes
- 1/4 cup diced green bell pepper
- 1 teaspoon ground cumin
- 1/2 teaspoon ground coriander
- Salt and black pepper to taste
- 2 tablespoons olive oil

For the Dough (Short crust):

- 2 1/2 cups all-purpose flour
- 1 cup (2 sticks) unsalted butter, cold and cubed
- 1/2 teaspoon salt
- 1/2 cup ice water

Filling Preparation

In a skillet, heat the olive oil over medium heat. Add the minced garlic and diced red onion, and sauté until they become softened and aromatic.

Add the ground lamb to the skillet and cook, breaking it apart with a spatula, until it's browned and fully cooked.

Stir in the diced tomatoes and diced green bell pepper. Cook for a few more minutes until the vegetables are tender.

Season the mixture with ground cumin, ground coriander, salt, and black pepper. Mix well to incorporate the spices.

Remove the skillet from heat and stir in the finely chopped fresh mint leaves. Adjust the seasonings to your taste.

Allow the lamb and mint filling to cool to room temperature before using it in your empanadas.

Dough Handling

If you're making your own dough, follow the instructions in Chapter 2 for making shortcrust dough. Divide the dough into equal portions and roll them into small balls.

Roll out each dough ball into a thin circle, approximately 6-8 inches in diameter, using a rolling pin and a lightly floured surface.

Place a spoonful of the lamb and mint filling in the center of each dough circle.

Fold the dough over the filling, creating a half-moon shape. Press the edges firmly to seal the empanada. You can use a fork to crimp the edges for a decorative touch.

Repeat this process for the remaining dough and filling.

Baking and Serving

Preheat your oven to 375°F (190°C).

Place the lamb and mint empanadas on a baking sheet lined with parchment paper, ensuring there is some space between them for even baking.

If desired, you can brush the tops of the empanadas with an egg wash (a beaten egg with a tablespoon of water) for a shiny, golden crust.

Bake the empanadas in the preheated oven for 20-25 minutes or until they are golden brown and the lamb filling is flavorful.

Allow the empanadas to cool for a few minutes before serving. They are best enjoyed warm.

Consider serving these exotic empanadas with a side of tzatziki sauce or a Greek salad for a Mediterranean-inspired feast.

Lamb and mint empanadas offer a taste of the exotic with the rich flavor of ground lamb and the refreshing, aromatic notes of fresh mint.

Chapter 12: South American Favorites: Argentine Beef Empanadas

Ingredients

For the Filling:

- 1 pound ground beef
- 1/2 cup diced yellow onion
- 1/4 cup diced green bell pepper
- 1/4 cup diced red bell pepper
- 2 cloves garlic, minced
- 1/4 cup pitted green olives, chopped
- 2 hard-boiled eggs, chopped
- 1/2 teaspoon ground cumin
- 1/2 teaspoon paprika
- Salt and black pepper to taste
- 2 tablespoons olive oil

For the Dough (Short crust):

- 2 1/2 cups all-purpose flour
- 1 cup (2 sticks) unsalted butter, cold and cubed
- 1/2 teaspoon salt
- 1/2 cup ice water

Filling Preparation

In a skillet, heat the olive oil over medium heat. Add the minced garlic, diced yellow onion, diced green bell pepper, and diced red bell pepper. Sauté until they become softened and fragrant.

Add the ground beef to the skillet and cook, breaking it apart with a spatula, until it's browned and fully cooked.

Stir in the chopped green olives, chopped hard-boiled eggs, ground cumin, paprika, salt, and black pepper. Mix well to incorporate all the ingredients.

Remove the skillet from heat and allow the beef filling to cool to room temperature before using it in your empanadas.

Dough Handling

If you're making your own dough, follow the instructions in Chapter 2 for making short crust dough. Divide the dough into equal portions and roll them into small balls.

Roll out each dough ball into a thin circle, approximately 6-8 inches in diameter, using a rolling pin and a lightly floured surface.

Place a spoonful of the Argentine beef filling in the center of each dough circle.

Fold the dough over the filling, creating a half-moon shape. Press the edges firmly to seal the empanada. You can use a fork to crimp the edges for a decorative touch.

Repeat this process for the remaining dough and filling.

Baking and Serving

Preheat your oven to 375°F (190°C).

Place the Argentine beef empanadas on a baking sheet lined with parchment paper, ensuring there is some space between them for even baking.

If desired, you can brush the tops of the empanadas with an egg wash (a beaten egg with a tablespoon of water) for a shiny, golden crust.

Bake the empanadas in the preheated oven for 20-25 minutes or until they are golden brown and the beef filling is savory and aromatic.

Allow the empanadas to cool for a few minutes before serving. They are best enjoyed warm.

Consider serving these South American favorites with a side of chimichurri sauce for an authentic Argentine experience.

Argentine beef empanadas are a beloved South American classic, featuring seasoned ground beef, colorful bell peppers, green olives, and hard-boiled eggs. These empanadas are a flavorful and satisfying treat that captures the essence of Argentina's culinary tradition.

Chapter 13: Caribbean Vibes: Jamaican Beef Patty Empanadas

Ingredients

For the Filling:

- 1 pound ground beef
- 1/2 cup diced onion
- 1/4 cup diced bell pepper (red, green, or yellow)
- 2 cloves garlic, minced
- 2 teaspoons Jamaican curry powder
- 1/2 teaspoon ground allspice
- 1/2 teaspoon thyme leaves
- 1/4 teaspoon cayenne pepper (adjust to your spice preference)
- Salt and black pepper to taste
- 2 tablespoons vegetable oil

For the Dough (Short crust):

- 2 1/2 cups all-purpose flour
- 1 cup (2 sticks) unsalted butter, cold and cubed
- 1/2 teaspoon salt
- 1/2 cup ice water

Filling Preparation

In a skillet, heat the vegetable oil over medium heat. Add the minced garlic and diced onion. Sauté until they become softened and fragrant.

Add the ground beef to the skillet and cook, breaking it apart with a spatula, until it's browned and fully cooked.

Stir in the diced bell pepper, Jamaican curry powder, ground allspice, thyme leaves, cayenne pepper, salt, and black pepper. Mix well to incorporate all the spices and flavors.

Allow the beef filling to cook for a few more minutes, ensuring the spices are evenly distributed and the mixture is aromatic. Taste and adjust the seasonings to your liking.

Remove the skillet from heat and let the Jamaican beef patty filling cool to room temperature before using it in your empanadas.

Dough Handling

If you're making your own dough, follow the instructions in Chapter 2 for making shortcrust dough. Divide the dough into equal portions and roll them into small balls.

Roll out each dough ball into a thin circle, approximately 6-8 inches in diameter, using a rolling pin and a lightly floured surface.

Place a spoonful of the Jamaican beef patty filling in the center of each dough circle.

Fold the dough over the filling, creating a half-moon shape. Press the edges firmly to seal the empanada. You can use a fork to crimp the edges for a decorative touch.

Repeat this process for the remaining dough and filling.

Baking and Serving

Preheat your oven to 375°F (190°C).

Place the Jamaican beef patty empanadas on a baking sheet lined with parchment paper, ensuring there is some space between them for even baking.

If desired, you can brush the tops of the empanadas with an egg wash (a beaten egg with a tablespoon of water) for a shiny, golden crust.

Bake the empanadas in the preheated oven for 20-25 minutes or until they are golden brown and the beef filling is savory and fragrant.

Allow the empanadas to cool for a few minutes before serving. They are best enjoyed warm.

Consider serving these Caribbean-inspired empanadas with a side of mango salsa or a cooling cucumber salad for a tropical twist.

Jamaican beef patty empanadas bring the flavors of the Caribbean to your plate with a savory blend of ground beef, Jamaican spices, and a flaky pastry crust.

Chapter 14: Filipino Twist: Adobo Chicken Empanadas

Ingredients
For the Filling:

- 1 pound boneless, skinless chicken thighs, diced into small pieces
- 1/2 cup diced onion
- 1/4 cup diced potatoes
- 1/4 cup diced carrots
- 2 cloves garlic, minced
- 1/4 cup soy sauce
- 1/4 cup vinegar (white or cane vinegar)
- 1/2 teaspoon black peppercorns
- 2 bay leaves
- Salt and black pepper to taste
- 2 tablespoons vegetable oil

For the Dough (Short crust):

- 2 1/2 cups all-purpose flour
- 1 cup (2 sticks) unsalted butter, cold and cubed
- 1/2 teaspoon salt
- 1/2 cup ice water

Filling Preparation

In a skillet, heat the vegetable oil over medium heat. Add the minced garlic and diced onion. Sauté until they become softened and fragrant.

Add the diced chicken to the skillet and cook until it's no longer pink and starts to brown.

Stir in the diced potatoes and diced carrots. Cook for a few more minutes until the vegetables start to soften.

Pour in the soy sauce and vinegar, and add the black peppercorns and bay leaves. Mix well to combine.

Reduce the heat to low, cover the skillet, and let the mixture simmer for about 15-20 minutes, or until the chicken is tender and the flavors meld together. Stir occasionally.

Taste the adobo chicken filling and adjust the seasoning with salt and black pepper as needed. Remove the bay leaves.

Allow the adobo chicken filling to cool to room temperature before using it in your empanadas.

Dough Handling

If you're making your own dough, follow the instructions in Chapter 2 for making short crust dough. Divide the dough into equal portions and roll them into small balls.

Roll out each dough ball into a thin circle, approximately 6-8 inches in diameter, using a rolling pin and a lightly floured surface.

Place a spoonful of the adobo chicken filling in the center of each dough circle.

Fold the dough over the filling, creating a half-moon shape. Press the edges firmly to seal the empanada. You can use a fork to crimp the edges for a decorative touch.

Repeat this process for the remaining dough and filling.

Baking and Serving

Preheat your oven to 375°F (190°C).

Place the adobo chicken empanadas on a baking sheet lined with parchment paper, ensuring there is some space between them for even baking.

If desired, you can brush the tops of the empanadas with an egg wash (a beaten egg with a tablespoon of water) for a shiny, golden crust.

Bake the empanadas in the preheated oven for 20-25 minutes or until they are golden brown and the adobo chicken filling is aromatic and flavorful.

Allow the empanadas to cool for a few minutes before serving. They are best enjoyed warm.

Consider serving these Filipino-inspired empanadas with a side of garlic fried rice or a simple cucumber and tomato salad for a delightful meal.

Adobo chicken empanadas offer a Filipino twist on a classic favorite, featuring tender chicken pieces marinated in a savory soy-vinegar sauce.

Chapter 15: Indian Fusion: Curry Vegetable Empanadas

Ingredients

For the Filling:

- 2 cups mixed vegetables (such as carrots, peas, potatoes, and green beans), diced
- 1/2 cup diced onion
- 2 cloves garlic, minced
- 1 teaspoon curry powder (adjust to your spice preference)
- 1/2 teaspoon ground turmeric
- 1/2 teaspoon ground cumin
- 1/2 teaspoon ground coriander
- 1/4 teaspoon cayenne pepper (adjust to your spice preference)
- 1/2 cup coconut milk
- Salt and black pepper to taste
- 2 tablespoons vegetable oil

For the Dough (Short crust):

- 2 1/2 cups all-purpose flour
- 1 cup (2 sticks) unsalted butter, cold and cubed
- 1/2 teaspoon salt
- 1/2 cup ice water

Filling Preparation

In a skillet, heat the vegetable oil over medium heat. Add the minced garlic and diced onion. Sauté until they become softened and aromatic.

Add the diced vegetables to the skillet and cook for a few minutes until they start to soften.

Stir in the curry powder, ground turmeric, ground cumin, ground coriander, and cayenne pepper. Mix well to coat the vegetables with the spices.

Pour in the coconut milk and stir to combine. Reduce the heat to low, cover the skillet, and let the mixture simmer for about 10-15 minutes, or until the vegetables are tender and the flavors meld together. Stir occasionally.

Taste the curry vegetable filling and adjust the seasoning with salt and black pepper to your liking.

Allow the filling to cool to room temperature before using it in your empanadas.

Dough Handling

If you're making your own dough, follow the instructions in Chapter 2 for making short crust dough. Divide the dough into equal portions and roll them into small balls.

Roll out each dough ball into a thin circle, approximately 6-8 inches in diameter, using a rolling pin and a lightly floured surface.

Place a spoonful of the curry vegetable filling in the center of each dough circle.

Fold the dough over the filling, creating a half-moon shape. Press the edges firmly to seal the empanada. You can use a fork to crimp the edges for a decorative touch.

Repeat this process for the remaining dough and filling.

Baking and Serving

Preheat your oven to 375°F (190°C).

Place the curry vegetable empanadas on a baking sheet lined with parchment paper, ensuring there is some space between them for even baking.

If desired, you can brush the tops of the empanadas with an egg wash (a beaten egg with a tablespoon of water) for a shiny, golden crust.

Bake the empanadas in the preheated oven for 20-25 minutes or until they are golden brown and the curry vegetable filling is aromatic and flavorful.

Allow the empanadas to cool for a few minutes before serving. They are best enjoyed warm.

Consider serving these Indian-inspired empanadas with a side of mango chutney or a cucumber raita for a fusion feast.

Curry vegetable empanadas bring a taste of India to this beloved pastry, featuring a medley of mixed vegetables cooked in aromatic curry spices and creamy coconut milk. These empanadas offer a delightful fusion of flavors and are perfect for those who love Indian cuisine.

Chapter 16: Tex-Mex Style: Beef and Bean Empanadas

Ingredients

For the Filling:

- 1 pound ground beef
- 1/2 cup diced onion
- 1/4 cup diced red bell pepper
- 1/4 cup diced green bell pepper
- 1/2 cup canned black beans, drained and rinsed
- 1/2 cup canned corn kernels, drained
- 2 cloves garlic, minced
- 1 teaspoon chili powder
- 1/2 teaspoon ground cumin
- 1/2 teaspoon paprika
- Salt and black pepper to taste
- 1/4 cup tomato sauce
- 1/4 cup shredded cheddar cheese
- 2 tablespoons vegetable oil

For the Dough (Short crust):

- 2 1/2 cups all-purpose flour
- 1 cup (2 sticks) unsalted butter, cold and cubed
- 1/2 teaspoon salt
- 1/2 cup ice water

Filling Preparation

In a skillet, heat the vegetable oil over medium heat. Add the minced garlic, diced onion, diced red bell pepper, and diced green bell pepper. Sauté until they become softened and fragrant.

Add the ground beef to the skillet and cook, breaking it apart with a spatula, until it's browned and fully cooked.

Stir in the canned black beans, canned corn kernels, chili powder, ground cumin, paprika, salt, and black pepper. Mix well to incorporate all the flavors.

Add the tomato sauce to the mixture and stir until everything is evenly coated. Simmer for a few more minutes until the filling is heated through.

Taste the beef and bean filling and adjust the seasonings as needed.

Remove the skillet from heat and let the filling cool to room temperature before using it in your empanadas.

Dough Handling

If you're making your own dough, follow the instructions in Chapter 2 for making short crust dough. Divide the dough into equal portions and roll them into small balls.

Roll out each dough ball into a thin circle, approximately 6-8 inches in diameter, using a rolling pin and a lightly floured surface.

Place a spoonful of the beef and bean filling in the center of each dough circle.

Sprinkle a bit of shredded cheddar cheese over the filling.

Fold the dough over the filling, creating a half-moon shape. Press the edges firmly to seal the empanada. You can use a fork to crimp the edges for a decorative touch.

Repeat this process for the remaining dough and filling.

Baking and Serving

Preheat your oven to 375°F (190°C).

Place the beef and bean empanadas on a baking sheet lined with parchment paper, ensuring there is some space between them for even baking.

If desired, you can brush the tops of the empanadas with an egg wash (a beaten egg with a tablespoon of water) for a shiny, golden crust.

Bake the empanadas in the preheated oven for 20-25 minutes or until they are golden brown and the beef and bean filling is savory and satisfying.

Allow the empanadas to cool for a few minutes before serving. They are best enjoyed warm.

Consider serving these Tex-Mex delights with a side of salsa or guacamole for an extra burst of flavor.

Beef and bean empanadas with a Tex-Mex twist combine the hearty flavors of ground beef, black beans, and corn, all seasoned with classic Tex-Mex spices. These empanadas are a perfect addition to your Tex-Mex menu, whether as a snack or a party appetizer.

Chapter 17: Elegant Appetizers: Mini Empanada Bites

Ingredients

For the Filling:

- 1/2 pound ground beef
- 1/2 cup diced onion
- 1/4 cup diced red bell pepper
- 1/4 cup diced green bell pepper
- 1/2 cup canned black beans, drained and rinsed
- 1/4 cup frozen corn kernels, thawed
- 1 clove garlic, minced
- 1/2 teaspoon chili powder
- 1/4 teaspoon ground cumin
- Salt and black pepper to taste
- 2 tablespoons vegetable oil

For the Dough (Short crust):

- 1 1/4 cups all-purpose flour
- 1/2 cup (1 stick) unsalted butter, cold and cubed
- 1/4 teaspoon salt
- 3-4 tablespoons ice water

Filling Preparation

In a skillet, heat the vegetable oil over medium heat. Add the minced garlic, diced onion, diced red bell pepper, and diced green bell pepper. Sauté until they become softened and fragrant.

Add the ground beef to the skillet and cook, breaking it apart with a spatula, until it's browned and fully cooked.

Stir in the canned black beans, thawed corn kernels, chili powder, ground cumin, salt, and black pepper. Mix well to combine all the flavors.

Allow the beef filling to cook for a few more minutes until the beans and corn are heated through.

Taste the filling and adjust the seasonings as needed.

Remove the skillet from heat and let the filling cool to room temperature before using it in your mini empanada bites.

Dough Handling

If you're making your own dough, follow the instructions in Chapter 2 for making short crust dough. Divide the dough into equal portions and roll them into small balls.

Roll out each dough ball into a thin circle, approximately 4-5 inches in diameter, using a rolling pin and a lightly floured surface.

Place a small spoonful of the beef filling in the center of each dough circle.

Fold the dough over the filling, creating a half-moon shape. Press the edges firmly to seal the mini empanada bite. You can use a fork to crimp the edges for a decorative touch.

Repeat this process for the remaining dough and filling.

Baking and Serving

Preheat your oven to 375°F (190°C).

Place the mini empanada bites on a baking sheet lined with parchment paper, ensuring there is some space between them for even baking.

If desired, you can brush the tops of the empanadas with an egg wash (a beaten egg with a tablespoon of water) for a shiny, golden crust.

Bake the mini empanada bites in the preheated oven for 15-20 minutes or until they are golden brown and the filling is heated through.

Allow the mini empanada bites to cool for a few minutes before serving. They are perfect bite-sized appetizers for elegant gatherings.

Consider serving these mini empanada bites with a dipping sauce of your choice, such as salsa, aioli, or a creamy cilantro lime sauce.

Mini empanada bites are a delightful addition to any elegant appetizer spread, offering a savory blend of ground beef, black beans, and sweet corn, all encased in a flaky pastry crust. These bite-sized treats are perfect for impressing your guests at special occasions.

Chapter 18: Empanada Sides and Dips

Salsa and Sauce Recipes
Classic Tomato Salsa
Ingredients:

- 2 cups diced tomatoes (fresh or canned)
- 1/2 cup diced onion
- 1/4 cup chopped fresh cilantro
- 2 cloves garlic, minced
- 1 jalapeño pepper, seeds removed and finely chopped (adjust to your spice preference)
- Juice of 1 lime
- Salt and black pepper to taste

Instructions:

1. In a bowl, combine diced tomatoes, diced onion, chopped cilantro, minced garlic, and chopped jalapeño pepper.
2. Squeeze the lime juice over the mixture and stir to combine.
3. Season with salt and black pepper to taste.
4. Allow the flavors to meld together in the refrigerator for at least 30 minutes before serving.

Creamy Avocado Dip
Ingredients:

- 2 ripe avocados, peeled, pitted, and mashed
- 1/4 cup sour cream
- 1/4 cup mayonnaise
- 2 cloves garlic, minced

- 1 tablespoon fresh lime juice
- Salt and black pepper to taste
- 1/4 teaspoon ground cumin (optional)

Instructions:

1. In a bowl, combine mashed avocados, sour cream, mayonnaise, minced garlic, and fresh lime juice.
2. Season with salt, black pepper, and ground cumin (if using) to taste.
3. Mix well until the dip is creamy and well combined.
4. Refrigerate for at least 30 minutes before serving.

Salad Pairings
Southwestern Corn and Black Bean Salad
Ingredients:

- 1 can (15 ounces) black beans, drained and rinsed
- 1 cup corn kernels (fresh or canned)
- 1 cup diced red bell pepper
- 1/2 cup diced red onion
- 1/4 cup chopped fresh cilantro
- 2 tablespoons olive oil
- Juice of 1 lime
- Salt and black pepper to taste

Instructions:

1. In a large bowl, combine black beans, corn kernels, diced red bell pepper, diced red onion, and chopped cilantro.
2. Drizzle olive oil and lime juice over the salad and toss to combine.
3. Season with salt and black pepper to taste.
4. Chill in the refrigerator for at least 30 minutes before serving.

Beverage Recommendations
Traditional Sangria
Ingredients:

- 1 bottle red wine (750 ml)
- 1/4 cup brandy
- 1/4 cup orange liqueur (such as Triple Sec)
- 1/4 cup fresh orange juice
- 1/4 cup fresh lemon juice
- 1/4 cup fresh lime juice
- 2 tablespoons sugar
- 1 orange, thinly sliced
- 1 lemon, thinly sliced
- 1 lime, thinly sliced
- 1 apple, diced
- 1 cup club soda (optional)

Instructions:

1. In a large pitcher, combine red wine, brandy, orange liqueur, fresh orange juice, fresh lemon juice, fresh lime juice, and sugar.
2. Stir until the sugar is dissolved.
3. Add the sliced oranges, lemons, limes, and diced apple to the pitcher.
4. Chill in the refrigerator for at least 2 hours before serving.
5. If desired, add club soda just before serving for a sparkling sangria.

These salsa and sauce recipes, salad pairings, and beverage recommendations are designed to complement your empanada experience. They offer a variety of flavors and textures to enhance your enjoyment of empanadas, making them suitable for casual meals and special occasions alike.

Chapter 19: Dessert Empanadas: Apple Cinnamon and Nutella

Ingredients

For the Apple Cinnamon Filling:

- 2 apples, peeled, cored, and diced
- 1/4 cup granulated sugar
- 1 teaspoon ground cinnamon
- 1/4 teaspoon nutmeg
- 1 tablespoon lemon juice
- 1 tablespoon cornstarch
- 1/4 cup water

For the Nutella Filling:

- 1/2 cup Nutella or chocolate hazelnut spread
- 1/4 cup chopped hazelnuts (optional)
- 1/4 cup mini chocolate chips (optional)

For the Dough (Short crust):

- 2 1/2 cups all-purpose flour
- 1 cup (2 sticks) unsalted butter, cold and cubed
- 1/2 teaspoon salt
- 1/2 cup ice water

Filling Preparation

For the Apple Cinnamon Filling:

- In a saucepan, combine diced apples, granulated sugar, ground cinnamon, nutmeg, lemon juice, cornstarch, and water.
- Cook over medium heat, stirring occasionally, until the apples

are soft and the mixture has thickened (about 10-15 minutes).

- Remove from heat and allow the apple cinnamon filling to cool completely before using it in your empanadas.

For the Nutella Filling:

- Simply scoop out Nutella or chocolate hazelnut spread into a bowl. If desired, you can add chopped hazelnuts and mini chocolate chips for extra texture and flavor.
- Mix well to combine all the ingredients. The Nutella filling is ready to use.

Dough Handling

If you're making your own dough, follow the instructions in Chapter 2 for making short crust dough. Divide the dough into equal portions and roll them into small balls.

Roll out each dough ball into a thin circle, approximately 6-8 inches in diameter, using a rolling pin and a lightly floured surface.

Filling and Assembling

For the Apple Cinnamon Empanadas:

- Place a spoonful of the cooled apple cinnamon filling in the center of each dough circle.

- Fold the dough over the filling, creating a half-moon shape. Press the edges firmly to seal the empanada. You can use a fork to crimp the edges for a decorative touch.

- Repeat this process for the remaining dough and apple cinnamon filling.

For the Nutella Empanadas:

- Place a spoonful of Nutella filling in the center of each dough circle.

- If you've added chopped hazelnuts and mini chocolate chips, sprinkle them over the Nutella filling.

- Fold the dough over the filling, creating a half-moon shape. Press the edges firmly to seal the empanada. You can use a fork to crimp the edges for a decorative touch.

- Repeat this process for the remaining dough and Nutella filling.

Baking and Serving

Preheat your oven to 375°F (190°C).

Place the dessert empanadas on a baking sheet lined with parchment paper, ensuring there is some space between them for even baking.

If desired, you can brush the tops of the empanadas with an egg wash (a beaten egg with a tablespoon of water) for a shiny, golden crust.

Bake the empanadas in the preheated oven for 20-25 minutes or until they are golden brown and the fillings are warm and gooey.

Allow the dessert empanadas to cool for a few minutes before serving. They are best enjoyed warm.

Dust the apple cinnamon empanadas with powdered sugar for an extra touch of sweetness, and serve the Nutella empanadas as they are.

Dessert empanadas offer a sweet ending to your meal with two delicious options: Apple Cinnamon Empanadas featuring spiced apple filling, and Nutella Empanadas filled with creamy chocolate hazelnut goodness. These dessert empanadas are perfect for satisfying your sweet tooth.

Congratulations on completing your journey through the "Empanada Cookbook"! You've explored a wide variety of empanada recipes, from classic savory fillings to sweet dessert options. Empanadas are a versatile and flavorful dish that can be enjoyed as appetizers, snacks, or even main courses. With this cookbook, you've learned how to create empanadas that cater to a range of tastes and occasions.

Throughout this cookbook, you've discovered:

Empanada Basics: You started with the foundations, learning about different types of empanada dough, both homemade and store-bought, and essential rolling and shaping techniques.

Savory Empanadas: You explored a diverse array of savory empanadas, from classic beef and chicken options to vegetarian, seafood, and breakfast varieties. You've also ventured into regional and international flavors, such as Jamaican beef patty and Argentine beef empanadas.

Cheese-Filled Empanadas: For cheese lovers, you indulged in empanadas featuring a variety of cheese fillings, from the creamy queso blanco to the spicy jalapeño and cheddar options.

Exotic Fillings: You delved into unique and exotic fillings like lamb and mint, offering a delightful twist on traditional empanadas.

Dessert Empanadas: To satisfy your sweet tooth, you explored dessert empanadas with delicious choices like apple cinnamon and Nutella, perfect for a sweet ending to any meal.

Sides and Dips: No empanada is complete without complementary sides and dips. You've discovered salsa and sauce recipes, refreshing salad pairings, and beverage recommendations to enhance your empanada experience.

As you've journeyed through the chapters, you've not only expanded your culinary skills but also gained the confidence to experiment with flavors and ingredients to create your own empanada masterpieces.

Remember that empanadas are a canvas for your creativity. You can mix and match fillings, experiment with different spices, and adapt them to your personal preferences. Whether you're sharing them with friends and family at a gathering or enjoying them as a comforting meal, empanadas are sure to be a crowd-pleaser.

Thank you for choosing this cookbook, and I hope it has inspired you to embark on a flavorful empanada-making adventure. May your kitchen be filled with the delightful aromas and delicious tastes of these savory and sweet pockets of joy. Happy cooking!